You Can Say "No" To Drugs!

A Drug-Free Kids Book

Gretchen Super
Illustrated by Blanche Sims

TWENTY-FIRST CENTURY BOOKS
FREDERICK, MARYLAND

Published by
Twenty-First Century Books
38 South Market Street
Frederick, Maryland 21701

Text Copyright © 1990
Twenty-First Century Books

Illustrations Copyright © 1990
Blanche Sims

Printed in the United States of America

10 9 8 7 6 5 4 3 2 1

Library of Congress Cataloging in Publication Data

Super, Gretchen
You Can Say "No" to Drugs!
Illustrated by Blanche Sims

(A Drug-Free Kids Book)
Includes bibliographical references.
Summary: Describes, in simple terms, how to say "No"
to drugs, how to listen to your own feelings, how to handle
peer pressure, and how to become a drug-free kid.
1. Drug abuse—prevention—Juvenile literature.
[1. Drug abuse—prevention.]
I. Sims, Blanche, ill. II. Title.
III. Series: Drug-Free Kids.
HV5801.S839   1990
613.8—dc20   90-31034 CIP AC
ISBN 0-941477-89-4

Table of Contents

Chapter 1

Saying "No" to Drugs

You are a drug-free kid.
You never use drugs.
You are proud to be
a drug-free kid.

And you want to stay
a drug-free kid.

You know that drugs are not safe.
You know that drugs hurt people.
Drugs hurt the people who use them.

They change the way people think.
They change the way people feel.
They change the way people act.

Drugs make people sick.
They hurt the body and brain.
And it can be hard for people to stop
using drugs once they start.

You know that drugs even hurt
people who do not use them.
Drugs hurt everyone.

You know the facts about drugs.
That's why you are a drug-free kid.
You want to say "No" to drugs.

As you get older, you may be asked
to use drugs.
Will you be able to say "No"?

Saying "No" to drugs sounds easy.
But sometimes it is not as easy
as it sounds.
Sometimes it is hard to say "No."

This book was written to help you
say "No" to drugs.
It will help you stay a drug-free kid.

Chapter 2

Making Your Own Decisions

"What clothes will I wear today?"

"What will I eat for breakfast?"

"Who will I sit next to at lunch?"

"What book will I pick from the library?"

You make many decisions everyday.
Some are easy to make.
Others can be very hard to make.

How do you decide what to do?
How do you make a decision?

Sometimes you get help from
the grown-up people you know.
Your Mom and Dad help you
decide what to do.
You get help from your
teachers, too.

Grown-up people make many
decisions for you.
They know what it is like to grow up.
They know that it is not always easy.
They know how to help you grow up
safe and happy.

But grown-ups can't make every
decision for you.
And they don't really want to.
They want you to learn how to make
your own decisions.
Learning to make your own decisions
is part of growing up.

You can help yourself
make a decision.
You can listen to what you
think is the right thing to do.
You can listen to what you
feel is the right thing to do.

Most of the time, you will know
what the right thing is.
You know it is wrong to lie or steal.
You know that other people think
it is wrong.
And you know it feels wrong inside.

How do you make a hard decision?

That's when you need to listen
to grown-ups.
Your parents and teachers will help
you do the right thing.

That's when you need to remember
what you have learned.
The things that you have learned
will help you do the right thing.

15

And that's when you
need to listen to yourself.
You know what is right for you.

Chapter 3

You and Your Peers

Have you ever seen older kids
smoking cigarettes?
You may have wondered:
"Why are they doing that?"
"Why are they using a drug?"
"Why are they hurting themselves?"

Some kids think using drugs is the
way to make friends.
This feeling is called "peer pressure."

What is a peer?

A peer is someone who is about
your own age.
Your peers are the kids who go
to school with you.

They are the kids who do the kinds
of things you do.
You want to be like your peers.
And you want your peers to like you.

Peer pressure is the feeling that you
have to do what your peers want to do.

Maybe you play the games that the
other kids want to play.
You do it because you don't want
to be left out.

Maybe you buy the same toys that
the other kids buy.
You do it because you want to be
part of the group.

Your peers may want you to do
something you don't really want to do.
Maybe you really want to play
a different game today.

But your peers want you to play the
game they want to play.
They might ask you again and again.
They might tease you over and over.

Your peers may want you to do
something you think is wrong.
They may want you to be mean
to other kids.
They may want you to take something
that doesn't belong to you.

It can be hard to say "No"
to your peers.

It can be hard to do
what you want to do.

It can be hard to do
what you think is right.

No one likes to be teased.
No one likes to be left out.

It can be hard to tell your peers "No."

But you can make the right decision.
You can do what is right for you.

Chapter 4

A Drug-Free You

Someday, you may be asked
to use drugs.
Your peers may ask you to use drugs.
They may tell you it is fun to use drugs.
They may tell you it is safe
to use drugs.

You will know what to do.
You will want to say "No."

When you say "No," your peers may
try to make you use drugs.
They may call you mean names.
They may try to make you feel
like a baby if you don't use drugs.
They may not talk to you anymore.

It can be hard to say "No" to drugs.
But most kids do say "No."
And they get lots of help to make
that decision.

Grown-up people help you say "No"
to drugs.

Remember the grown-up people who
love and care for you.
Remember what they have told you
about drugs.
They want you to be safe and happy.
They want you to say "No" to drugs.

Friends help each other say "No"
to drugs.

Remember that your friends
care about you.
Real friends will not try to make
you use drugs.
They want you to be drug-free.
Using drugs is no way to make friends.

You can help yourself say "No" to drugs.

Remember what you have learned
about drugs.
You know that using drugs
will hurt you.
You know that it is against the law
for you to use drugs.
You know that you will hurt the
people who love you if you use drugs.
You know that using drugs is wrong.

Listen to your own feelings.
You want to be happy.
You want to be healthy.
You want to be safe.
You want to be smart.

You want to be
proud of yourself.
You want to be
the best you can be.

The best you is
a drug-free you.
Be proud to be
a drug-free kid.

Remember one more thing:
     You can do it!
You can say "No" to drugs!

Chapter 5

Ways to Say "No"

Saying "No" to drugs is a big job.
Here are ways to help you say "No."

- If someone asks you to use drugs,
  say "No."

You could say "No way" or "Forget it."
You could also say:

"No. I don't want to hurt myself."
"No. Using drugs is stupid."
"No. It's against the law."

There are many ways to say "No."
Find a way to say "No"—and say it.

- If someone asks you to use drugs, walk away.

Say "No" and just walk away.
Do not talk to that person.
Do not argue with that person.
Just walk away.

- If someone asks you to use drugs,
  tell a grown-up.

Say "No," walk away, and find a
grown-up you can talk to.
A grown-up needs to know
what happened.
A grown-up can help you.

It is against the law for kids
to use drugs.
If someone asks you to use drugs,
they are breaking the law.
If other kids ask you to use drugs,
they want you to break the law, too.
A grown-up will know what to do.

Being a drug-free kid is a big job.
Here are some ways to help you
stay drug-free.

- Make friends with other drug-free kids.

- Learn more about what drugs are
  and what they do.

- Talk to your parents or teachers about drugs.

- Stay away from places where drugs are used.

- Don't be afraid to ask questions about drugs.

- Start a "Drug-Free Kids" club in your school.

Staying drug-free is a big job.
But you can do it.
You can make your life a drug-free one.

Chapter 6

A Drug-Free World

You hear a lot about drugs.
You may be worried about drugs.
You may think everyone uses drugs.

But the fact is that most people
never use drugs.

Look around you.
You know lots of drug-free people.

Look at the grown-ups you know.
Look at the other kids you know.
Many grown-ups never use drugs.
Most kids never use drugs.
Most kids stay drug-free.

You are a drug-free kid.
You can stay a drug-free kid, too.
You get lots of help to stay drug-free.
And you can help yourself.

Let's work together
to say "No" to drugs.
Let's make our lives drug-free.
Let's make our world drug-free.

We can do it!

Words You Need to Know

Being a drug-free kid is a big job. But you can do it. Knowing about drugs will help you stay drug-free. Here are some words you need to know.

addicted	when someone can't stop using drugs
alcohol	a drug found in drinks like beer and wine
cocaine	a drug that comes from the coca plant
crack	a kind of cocaine that is smoked
drug	something that changes the way the body and brain work
joint	a marijuana cigarette
marijuana	a drug that comes from the cannabis plant
medicine	the kind of drug a doctor gives you when you are sick
nicotine	a drug found in things made from the tobacco plant
peer pressure	when other people make you feel that you have to do something
poison	something that hurts the body if you eat or drink it

Index

Drugs and Our Children

A Note to Parents, Teachers, and Librarians

Drug-Free Kids is a book series for children ages 5 to 8. Our children, even at this early age, hear about drugs, but they may not understand what the drug problem is about. They know that drugs are a problem. But they may not know why or how.

This series was written to help young children understand why and how drugs are a problem. Drug-Free Kids places the problem of drug use within a framework of issues children may already know about—issues such as health and wellness, social responsibility, and personal choice. The need to say "No" to drugs is presented not as a question separate from the other important decisions our children have to face, but as one part of an outlook on life that enables them to grow up happy and healthy.

These books are designed to encourage independent reading. But no book series on drugs can take the place of active adult involvement in the lives of our children. I hope you will take the time to read these books with your children or students. They will have questions, and you may not have all the answers. But Drug-Free Kids gives us an excellent start. It opens a dialogue on one of the most important challenges of our time: how to teach our children to say "No" to drugs.

Lee Dogoloff, Executive Director
American Council for Drug Education